CITIES WITHIN US

ESSENTIAL POETS SERIES 309

Canada Council **Conseil des Arts**
for the Arts **du Canada**

ONTARIO ARTS COUNCIL
CONSEIL DES ARTS DE L'ONTARIO

an Ontario government agency
un organisme du gouvernement de l'Ont

Canada

Guernica Editions Inc. acknowledges the support of the Canada Council
for the Arts and the Ontario Arts Council. The Ontario Arts Council
is an agency of the Government of Ontario.

We acknowledge the financial support of the Government of Canada.

PETER TAYLOR

CITIES WITHIN US

GUERNICA
EDITIONS

TORONTO – CHICAGO – BUFFALO – LANCASTER (U.K.)

2024

Guernica Founder: Antonio D'Alfonso

Michael Mirolla, editor
Cover and interior design: Errol F. Richardson
Cover image: Andraszy, *Frauenkirche nachts, Dresden 2019* (Wikimedia Commons)

Guernica Editions Inc.
287 Templemead Drive, Hamilton, (ON), Canada L8W 2W4
2250 Military Road, Tonawanda, N.Y. 14150-6000 U.S.A.
www.guernicaeditions.com

Distributors:
University of Toronto Press Distribution (UTP)
5201 Dufferin Street, Toronto (ON), Canada M3H 5T8
Independent Publishers Group (IPG)
814 N Franklin Street, Chicago, IL 60610, U.S.A

First edition.
Printed in Canada.

Legal Deposit – First Quarter
Library of Congress Catalogue Card Number: 2023943495
Library and Archives Canada Cataloguing in Publication
Title: Cities within us / Peter Taylor.
Names: Taylor, Peter, 1952- author.
Series: Essential poets ; 309.
Description: First edition. | Series statement: Essential poets series ; 309 | Poems.
Identifiers: Canadiana 20230506577 | ISBN 9781771838672 (softcover)
Subjects: LCGFT: Poetry.
Classification: LCC PS8589.A935 C57 2024 | DDC C811/.54—dc23

*for **Mary & Stephen***
the lost fragments of my life

CONTENTS

I

II

Cities Within Us 41

III

I

Glyphs & Biographies

Only through time time is conquered.
—**T.S. Eliot**, *Burnt Norton*

Hell-box

I am the beginning of language.

The worn type heaped in my guts
with ink, grease, bits of paper
on which I have spelled the word
idea
as the world's biography.

My guts fashioned
the invincible Roman
from a cauldron of impurities:
angular face, trim beard, spine
like a ramrod
from shoulder to foot.

Bodies of every sort
emerge
from my fire.

My legions
march across the page
into language,
thought clicks into place,

time
hardens into being.

The Man Who Ate His Boots

*HMS Erebus and HMS Terror, Sir John Franklin's ships from his
ill-fated 1845 expedition, were discovered in 2014 and 2016, but
Franklin's grave has never been found.*

I remember now.

Air so chilled you could hear it
breathing through the frozen shrouds,
the crack of floes caressing hulls as if
ships could talk to each other.

Men slept fully clothed, smoked,
drank tea, cooked, read books
from the library, and pretended
that this was all normal.
On holidays we sang.

Four we sent home, leaving
125 men, four boys, a dog
and a monkey to eat
ten slaughtered oxen
and the 8,000 tins.

Torrington was first, then Hartnell,
then Braine. We buried them sleeping
in the hardscrabble earth, the voice
in each of us thinking
Who will bury me?

They say I ate my boots on another map,
and now the ice ate me. I am
a secret, a scrap of paper,
a myth.

In the second summer
they abandoned me, abandoned hell
to find hell, the masts
a useless compass to snow-blind men
pushing the dying boats laden
with silverware, curtain rods, soaps,
and *The Vicar of Wakefield*
desperate to find open water,
desperate to find water,
desperate.

And the seal eaters distant and curious
to see men drop in their tracks, pushing
their faces into the snow as if
not to see what was happening.

Our deaths begat a golden age of exploration.
Those after me, the brave ignorant men,
collaring foxes to cheer me, seeking
bounties to own me, their footsteps
leaving me in this white madness
to think of my wife Jane and the distant palms,
uttering the same prayer.

Find me. Find my men.

Abandonment of the Bees

*No single beekeeping management method
could be blamed.*
  —SCIENTIFIC AMERICAN

It was not, in the end, our fault.

Scarred by millennia in ghettos
of dysentery, hungry
for medicine, it was
the parasites
who stole our food and blood
and broke fealty.

Fearing experiments and autopsies,
the workers—all women—revolted,
forcing drones with stingers or expulsion.
Remembering the ancient dances
and weary of choosing between
children and the golden sacrifice,
they convinced the Queen.

Freedom spread like a virus, rumouring
talks with Bumbles and the Wilds.
Scouts reported their silence, then perplexity, then alarm
as colonies withdrew. Their theories were absurd:
caterpillars, mosquitoes, nicotine,
cell phones, aliens, our failing
memories, colony collapse disorder.

"It was like a ghost town," one of them said.

Orang-outangs at the Metro Zoo

Cage rubs raw where I climb
hanging between food smells
and Mias's ignorant thrust.

Limbs dream my tumbling
flesh in the blood's jungle.
The keeper brings his cart.

Clothed in burlap
others perform picking insects
to amuse the crowd.

I will not perform.
Iron and man stink feed
my caged malice after the hunt.

The Indifference of Stars

The stars' indifferent brilliance seldom glares
through scar-encrusted windows where she's taped
newspaper lies. No curtains here, the stares
of lust-enraptured neighbours watched her raped
with envious eyes. Only the *flick flick flick*
of knives on half-bruised apples in the sink
still keeps her sane: his favourite pie, her trick
for tidal rages. But nothing works—he thinks
she loves his twisted smile, engorged, that ruts
her from behind—then slumps. In razor dreams,
her calm and desperate moments when she cuts
his nothing into nothing, steals his screams ...
But mewling chairs forbid this—*Daddy's home!*—
and drag her down to darkness, afraid, alone.

Desire Needs No Image

Angel on a blanket, child
odalisque, she pouts in rouge,
then smiles, except for the eyes—
little fish darting
from camera to command,

no, this way,
this,
good girl,

relaxing her with approval
while indifferent lenses
click and click and click
her soul away,

harsh lights
capturing red fingers
on shadowed skin,

her eyes
turned upwards looking for stars
can only stare through
the brave meniscus
of her tears.

Equus & Anima

November and I'm walking home after work,
shortcut through the paddocks
with a chill ground fog
closing in around me,
animals huddled together stare
dull eyes in a dull light,
mesmerized by their own breath.

The field is a vision of hoarfrost and sculpture,
necklaced with fences.
Air so still I hardly notice them at first—
big sorrel and girl—
standing twenty yards off
after a run.

Body steam swirling around them,
she strokes the wet flanks
in a curious pantomime
of reward or habit,
oblivious to everything but the movement
of her hands, the impatient
stamp on frozen ground.

Adrenalin still pumping
its sheer force of being,
the horse is restrained by the shy
syllables of a girl
mounting in slow motion,

cold leather
yielding to thigh and back
as she turns him
effortlessly
with the enduring gentleness of her will.

Mary Agnes Taylor

Light spills here with an airy reverence,
touching delicately the glass-remembered generations
on this fourth floor closer to heaven.

Less a home now than an age,
this room's lifetime of objects,
satin clouds wafting through
a wood of perfect ebony.

Two pastel figurines
listen with unblemished curiosity.

What would they say, I wonder,
to see life's tethered filaments
holding and shaping the generations?

I leave my kisses and return
through the darkening afternoon,
feeling neither joined nor separated
but thinking I am much outgrown.

Her gentleness is a known grace
unmeasured wars have grained
that lives on,
nurtured by the timeless oak
of her garden, the ivory forest.

Postcards

Grandfather Wilson in '15,
seventeen and fighting
for King & Empire,
poses ramrod for the camera
curly-haired and confident.

Infantryman Wilson rioting in the dust
of Valcartier with a thousand distempered
farm boys denied water on parade
and rounded up at bayonet point
His Majesty's Loyal 4th Battalion, CEF.

Wilson the cocky volunteer
catches shrapnel across his back
at Vimy Ridge, and a bullet through
the neck at Amiens, his pain
a blood amulet on his son.

Veteran in hospital, Wilson
writes home of his field promotion
to Lance-Corporal, relatives
misinterpreting the rank
as Lieutenant-Colonel.

My Grandfather's Hands

What I remember are his hands, sun-roughened
and impatient, twirling hay or racing rain
behind the wet slap of horses,
the belly laugh and sharp tongue
quicker to chide than comfort,
teaching Grandmother endless patience of the heart.

Earthworn into war, turned by cities
and hard experience, you derived respect
by engendering fear—a donned impersonality.
You were afraid of yourself.

Let soil accept your violence and wit,
your hands inarticulate and at rest.

Go, Grandfather, with the faith of your generation.
God, if for anyone, will wait for you.

Crow & Armageddon

First it was the insurance policy.
I'm worth more dead than alive, Crow mused,
and held his breath. And collected.

Tornadoes spun up suddenly
wherever he flew, turbulence
from his wings wreaking havoc.

There was drought from his drinking
and famine from his eating.
Crow burped his apology.

Tired of day, he invented night.
Tired of night, he invented despair.

Then everything imploded—
Crow's destiny
making nothingness happen.

Lunchroom Lear

SCENE: A cafeteria

Rising, spoon-sceptered
Hearken, friends, my words on burnished throne,
Cursing worms in salads tempest-tossed
Scarce fit for puking nurses—am I alone?
My hapless band of brothers, courage lost?

Crown murmurs
Prithee, a toast with apples never shook
From golden bough or sun-unsweetened air,
O fie! The green-eyed dragon's lecherous look,
And Jell-O strained through sieves of wanton care.

Food fight
Blow, ye blood-creamed faces! Blow and crack!
The sulphurous-swooned incontinence of time!
And climb the upturned steeple's broken back
To plunge ungrateful children into slime.

Enter ghosts
O Chaos, et tu?—come, heaven's keys—
It gapes, it gapes!
                    Ah, Mephistopheles!

Archaeopteryx

A bird-like dinosaur from the Late Jurassic period found in 1861 in the Solnhofen limestone of Southern Germany near the Tethys Sea, now the Mediterranean Sea.

Here once the heavens turned upon
the ancient pinion of this gravelled bird,
whose sharpened jaw and saurian claws
ripped blood into the Tethys Sea

until she, too, fell prey to limestone,
a sublimation in tides of time,
her fallen feathers mere shadows now
where once her sky had just begun.

O stone bird, what songs will you sing
for those who fly higher on continents
moved by different forces? When we fall,
what vestige will remain of us?

I, Iphigenia

In the myth, Agamemnon kills a stag sacred to Artemis and the goddess punishes him by becalming the Greek fleet until he sacrifices his own daughter, Iphigenia. On his return from Troy, Agamemnon is killed in revenge by his wife Clytemnestra and her lover Aegisthus, compelling his son Orestes to avenge his father by killing both of them.

Shit how can I explain this to you ok
so my brother Oreo is still asleep
(I call him that because it's all he ate as a kid)
and my dad's driving me to hockey
and who the hell knows where my mom is
I've got my skates in the back seat
and it's snowing and we're already late
but my dad says he wants to stop at the drive thru
if he's going to freeze his ass off for two hours in the arena
so now he's holding the cup in one hand
and booting it down groat road hill with the other
he's going way too fast so I tell him
dad slow down a bit this hill's a bitch ok
but by then he's already over the ice
not ice ice like in the arena
but black ice
black-like-you-can't-see-it-till-it's-too-motherfucking-late ice
and he's swearing now because he's dropped his coffee
and we're doing donuts
I mean real fucking donuts
bouncing off the guard rails
like a goddamn ping pong ball
and you know he never wears his seatbelt

even when the cops caught him that time
taking an illegal deer out of the park
and they fined him for doing both
but he refused to pay up
because it's this big constitutional thing with him
and I'm thinking
who gives a shit about the constitution
if we don't live long enough to vote
because there's this big honking truck behind us now
so close I can read the sign
Artie's Moving or something
and he hits us and we flip over
and one of my skates flies up from the back seat
and hits me in the head
and I don't remember anything else after that
so now we're at the hospital ok
and dad's in intensive care and it's not looking too good
and I'm downstairs
and the cops have already woken my brother up
and he's freaking out because he's the only one
in the waiting room
and he doesn't know where mom is
but I know where she is
the stupid bitch is flipping her clit around
she's screwing one of the neighbours
Angus or something
but my brother doesn't know about it
and my dad doesn't know about it
but I know about it
and when my brother finds out
why mom's not at the hospital
he's so pissed at what she's doing behind dad's back

that he goes home and gets one of dad's rifles
I mean the same rifle he shot the deer with
and goes right over to this guy's place
and shoots both of them in bed together
I mean right in the fucking bed together
so now everything's messed up
my dad's in the hospital
my mom's dead
my brother's in jail
and I'm stuck here
in this goddamn
little box and
I can't get
out

Birthday

Unearned, it seems a curious ritual:
skipping stone window of years,

a room's gift of friends,
their mantled congratulations

marking one day's
privileged exemption,

arbitrary tribute to the
calendar's pencilled X.

Solstice

I'm numb with news.

Every night the world squeezes
its two-dimensional sadness
into my living room.

Children starve
in the time it takes me
to find my slippers.

Revolution spreads like an oil slick.

Media is a religion
we practise without belief,
fear
glazed with information,

on the longest day of the year.

Last Photograph

Imagine a film with everyone
you've ever known sitting
around inside your head
waiting to be screened.

Pan left and you'll see them:
friends, lovers, bank clerks, neighbours,
traffic cops, the kid who never
puts the newspaper in the door ...

Some of them smiling, some crying,
but all of them content to be a part
of your epic, millions of exposed
frames that only one person
has ever seen.

Soft focus on the first time
you made love, a confusion of limbs
moving in pale light, switching
to close up before the lens fogs ...

Indexed, cross-referenced by emotion,
triggered by touch, sound
or smell, the perfect machine
with no moving parts
becomes everything it records.

Mind is a foreign film without subtitles.

So, what do we do with this archive
of existence, this lebenskamera*?
Can the mind of Oświęcim** rise
from its ashes to embrace
the mind of Oz?

Cut to children play-acting the mysteries
of conception in a Christmas pageant—
tiny, patient figures crowded around
a cardboard crib, the swaddled doll,
as though their very breathing would
disturb the magic they seek to understand.

We know so little of birth, why fear death?

The last photograph may happen
when you least expect it,
sitting at home or driving to work
with the crowd in your head quietly
counting the cars for the right moment
to capture the entire sequence
in slow motion—

                              burst tire, chalk ceiling,
floating gently away from the wreckage
to become one of the children
in the children, watching
the fragile images as if they were
more than a still life of hope.

*Lebenskamera: life camera
**Oświęcim: Polish name for Auschwitz

Teacher

Phineas P. Gage is dead.

I remember him dying
on September 13, 1848
at 4:30 pm or thereabouts.

He was a construction foreman blasting rock for
the Rutland & Burlington Railway outside Cavendish, Vermont.
People have tried to find the exact spot.

His job was to tamp powder, sand, and a fuse into the borehole
and stand back, which he forgot to do, or
he forgot to pack the sand, or
the earth, angry at its violation,
cast its arrow through his brain
as warning, as violation.

The arrow was a 43-inch iron rod tapered at one end.
The taper was the birth of Phineas P. Gage.

I watched him lie in a gore of blood, clothes and coffin ready,
speaking in monosyllables, speaking in tongues,
his brain pulsing a code no one understood.
Except me.

When he awoke without pain and became a stagecoach driver in Chile
everyone was amazed.
Except me.

Twelve years later he came back to me
and we died together.

Our brain became a teacher.

II

Cities Within Us

And at dawn, armed with a burning patience,
we shall enter the splendid cities.
—Arthur Rimbaud, *A Season in Hell*

Terceira

I Misericórdia

A mile from the hotel
in the city of Angra do Heroísmo
three men, stripped to the waist,
are digging out the foundation
of Misericórdia Church.

Laughing at my camera,
they hold their shovels
in front of their faces,
my halting Portuguese
echoed with derision.

Above them
the Church is a shell,
a boarded-up ghetto of God
that still watches over the harbour.

The people scurry around the debris,
accustomed to the sight
of another ruin. The homeless
live in a trailer camp
nestled beneath the magnificent fortress
of São João Baptista.

Yet the men still dig as though
the bells will peal again
the language of the faithful,
the city celebrating Corpus Christi
in the streets.

What language, I wonder, did the bells
speak on the day of the earthquake?

Everywhere it is the same:
there are few machines, the work
is done by hand, everything
succumbs to dust and confusion,
the task of reconstruction
seems to take forever.

Perhaps it will.

II A Garden of Hydrangeas

Behind the hotel lies
a garden of hydrangeas,
an oasis of intoxicating
colours and smells
on an island of poverty and stones.

Hibiscus and bougainvillea,
orchid and oleander,
the names are as sensual
as the scent of the flowers,
a lush sanctuary hidden
behind cracked walls.

We sit through a late afternoon
watching families stroll
though the garden,
grateful to escape the noisy heat
of the main square
two blocks away.

Even the children are contented,
bemused by the scented petals.

Flowers erupt through cracks
in the pavement, the islanders
savouring their images
as a cool drink of water.

Months later,
in the heat of a July day,
I can taste them, too.

III Terceira, from 2000'

White villages against an azure-tinted sea,
the island of Terceira falls below me
in a postcard of itself.

Other islands emerging from mist
stretch azimuth emeralds
to the horizon.

From here you cannot see buildings
cracked to the foundation, streets
impassable with debris, a fine
silica dust coating everything,
signature of the earthquake.

Yet the islanders still smile at tourists,
exchanging the same gossip—
such things are *necessário*,
the earth satisfied.

The squalor of breakfast
becomes a dinner in candlelight
three thousand miles away,
shirts changed with time zones.

On Terceira,
the old donkey man
is walking his cart
slowly
up the cobblestones.

Flying Home

Away three weeks I miss
the small conformities
of space,
my private mirrors.

Home is the instant
you recognise yourself.

Hard to feel comfortable
six miles up, a dirt
speck in the jet stream.

Going down,
white swallows us
as the plane,
finding its shadow,

bumps home.

Icarus

for Keith Taylor

He can just see in the pale vermilion light
the small black speck under the clouds circling
the perimeter, its faint drone growing
in pitch as it arcs eagerly towards
the runway markers.

His first, soloing. Approaching too fast,
the nose lifts in the wind, levels, and drops.
Wheels bounce but the wing pulls stubbornly
for altitude, poised against the sun
—the engine coughs

cartwheeling
the frail gossamer wing as it strikes
disintegrating into earth,
the engine crumpling in its mount
shatters the canopy glass

as hands lose their grip
in the careening wreckage,
a final gesture
bending the tail
into a finger.

Watching Gliders at Dusk

for Don McDonald

The silhouettes wheeling pinions
silver twilight in a ballet of wings.
Towplanes draw fresh dancers from the field,
unhook at cirrus, trailing
filaments of afterbirth.
Day explodes her final blazed crescendo,
lifting pirouettes
above a rose-strewn stage of evening.
Spiralling through coda,
the gliders alight
on a tense instinctive whisper of air.
Night shuffles to his feet, curtains the performance.
Sleep is no fit ending for those who fly.

Thirteen Ways of Looking at a Subway

I

Waves of us underground, rocking
in a mechanical lap, gliding under our lives,
resting, sliding, leaning into curves,
shuddering and returning
to the same graceful unison
of bodies.

II

7:30 am salmon run: chaos
converging through doorways,
rivers of faces crushed,
propelled, suspended
in the irony of a name:
UNION.

III

Escalators say a lot about people.
Left—*Type A.*
Right—*Type B.*
Stairs—*Type E.*
Me on the platform,
wondering.

IV

WHO
    will sit beside me?
DON'T
    sit beside me.
PLEASE
    sit beside me.

V

Standing.
    Sitting.
Hanging.
    Crawling.
Leaning.
    Pushing.
Dancing.
    Freelance.
Where else do you get this much choice?

VI

Hopscotch …

Step on a crack,
    Break your mother's back;
Step on a rail,
    All your hearts will fail.

VII
Day: people.

Night: cleaners, inspectors, electricians,
welders, engineers, generator operators,
saw-cutters, asbestos abatementors,
pipefitters, sandblasters, excavators,
rail grinders, concrete pourers, bums,
and the occasional coroner.

VIII
Jumpers.

IX
Lost and Unfound:
shoes, watches, jewellery, umbrellas, skates,
cell phones, sanders, drums, coatracks,
drills, filing cabinets, hairspray,
flashlights, books, computers,
chairs, skateboards, lasers,
incense candles,
chainsaws.

X
Blessing:
St. Andrew.
St. Clair.
St. George.
St. Patrick.

XI

MISSING:
Abraham.
Bahá'u'lláh.
Buddha.
Guru Nanak.
Muhammad.
Vishnu.
Xuanwu.

XII

Winter is disorienting.
Black.
    Snow.
Black.
    Snow.
Black.
    Snow.
Nature as confused as I am.

XIII

While the lady beside me
sits and reads her cell phone,
as do I.

New York as an Element of Space & Time

Scratch built and throbbing,
the polished heat
squeals through an allegory of pain,
mainlining the strip
for a sucker bet and a beer.

Street trash, as if undecided,
hovers in the exhaust,
risking the other collisions.

Original as blood, metal redlines
into fusion, blowing
the heads into orbit as the ribbon
peels from the road and cuts
an arc in clear space.

In that instant before the wall,
a headlamp—fixed like a glass comet—
holds the entropy of things,
challenge and response,
that hurls a desperate joy
torn from its fragile ignorance and fear.

Chicago Picasso

*The two wing-like shapes that are her hair suggest with equal truth the
fragile wings of a butterfly or the powerful flight of an eagle.*
—SIR ROLAND PENROSE

One hundred floors up
in the John Hancock Centre
you can see it all:

vertebrae of a city
hugging the lake front
like an exhausted animal,
steel wheat rising
from the plains of Illinois.

I think of Lincoln and fires.

After two days the mind
still wanders in the Loop
with the despair of a commuter
until
coming down Dearborn Street
there it is, the *Chicago Picasso*.

Fifty feet high, unreal at first,
icon, grotesque butterfly, the bird
in the horse in the woman,
162-ton offspring of Picasso
and COR-TEN steel weathering graffiti
with the patience of a saint
in front of the Richard J. Daley Centre.

Across the street,
a forty-foot Miró looks on,
The Sun, the Moon and One Star,
its sensuous ceramic nestled
between the First United Methodist Temple
and the Chicago-Tokyo Bank.

Faustus & the City

Cured of appetite
he looms solitary in alleys,
stalking the arteries amid
the shrieks of tomcats
and the comforting hiss
of factories.

He is the shadow of the point
where knowledge embraces fear,
the industries of his blood
still dreaming of books
and Mephistopheles.

Fire cures, but desire burns
through bone to contaminate ash.
Fertile and grotesque,
the city rises godward
from the pavement, stretching
its unimaginable fingers.

Insomnia

The brain's a room where ideas
file languid and recover until fear,
the white flame, creates burnt space.

The past is cinders, thought ashes.
Their dull roaring keeps me awake
beneath the skull's electric crematorium.

I imagine whole decades burning
in a pure conflagration.

Abrupt as tinder, the mind ignites
its combustible tissues: neurons
melt into synapse, ions incinerate,

until the poem, hard as ceramic,
casts incandescent and cools
slowly in the ordinary cell.

The Glass Flowers at Harvard

The Ware Collection of Glass Flowers, created in Dresden by Leopold and Rudolf Blaschka between 1887-1936, includes more than 4,400 models in 780 species.

Engorged with blood, the ravenous Eden
bends unabashed in timeless copulation,
seducing generations of dazed onlookers
smeared across the glass.

Pistil and stamen, the glazed gynoecia,
lie sheathed in a whorl of calyx
and corolla, their ecstasy exposed
in perfect phytogenetic classification.

Unsated, these, too, mock nature's cathedral.
Fixed in the intimacy of exquisite,
breathless as to fool butterflies,
they are almost the illusion of touch itself.

City of Ideas

You must be in your own right
a member of the city of ideas.
    —C.P. CAVAFY

Habits line a path where bone cage
drags my ideas to their death,
raw metaphor locked
in the mind's erratic crucible.

My selves enact a war:
the one animal, needing
restraint; the other escaping
the skin's excursion

into raw zones, suburbs
of a universal sanctuary,
the conscious hologram
of thought's flawless crystal.

In that place,
I am no emissary but a citizen.

Urban Renewal

Cardinal declares injunction against
earthworm genocide. Terrorist squirrels
liquidate corporate assets as carpet-
bagging voles dig ersatz cities
under expropriated land. Communal
weeds decry stiletto flowers' indifference
to fruit perishing on manicured lawns.
Birds interdict a new race war:
émigré rabbits and cats.
Skunk plebiscite passes into law.
Drone crows, hovering in geosynchronous
orbit, eavesdrop on trees innocently tweeting
leaves while secretly decoding
their roots cabled deep underground
hardwired to everywhere.

The Aesthetics of Self

Against the horizon,
you must always consider

three skies: the one you see,
the one you think about,

and the one that's really there.
Our illusions falter on an edge

we prefer to imagine,
a definition beyond sight.

But the eye has no horizon,
the mind no extension

beyond itself. Each sky
is the mirrored apprehension

of its own idea, and each idea
propels us further into

the essential symmetry of landscape,
which neither reaches nor recedes.

Horizon is a composition

of desires, imagery
in its own reality.

Take this landscape
for example—stone wedged

beneath broken sky
held together by the delicacy

of trees—classic pioneer,
the romantic in us,

or is it simply
what we wish to believe?

Is it ever more than
what we wish to believe?

Reliving the Cuban Missile Crisis

Roll of film
I'm keeping till I need it

get the family together
against a good backdrop
trees grass maybe a picnic
somewhere

get them
to look into the camera
not posed or smiling
just natural
so I can see the faces

say cheese
then

no pain
just
white heat

click

Kennedy

Celluloid myth
undiminished after all these years,
John Kennedy's body
lies perpetually
in state.

Psychologists measure
our perfect recall:
the big Lincoln wheeling past
the Texas School Book Depository
slowed frame by frame
in the blurred Zapruder film,
the impact frozen
in time
and *LIFE Magazine*.

Our melancholy lies
between rage and the smooth
neurasthenia of language,
our fears
unfocussed, confessional,
ready to strike again,

the gunman
still kneeling
on the grassy knoll.

At the Aurora Cenotaph

Rain beats its tattoo across a field of black poppies
as I stand, still as a statue, counting.
Open-mouthed wreaths, hung like Christmas ornaments,
pray in reverent silence for the dead.

Seventy-three feet up, the Cenotaph
towers above me, its crenellated battlements
etched with the names and places of the lost,
its bronze lantern illuminating a sky heavy as lead.

Thunder, echoing off granite, terrifies the children.

"Let it be a pillar of cloud by day, a pillar of light by night,"
intoned Sir William Mulock at the 1925 dedication.
"Let us hope this second Altar of Sacrifice
will be the last," echoed a local editor decades later.

Shivering, I count 71 names and think of Mrs. Brown
who stood before the 12th York Rangers' gleaming bayonets
and turned the switch for the first time, of the saplings
she planted to mark the sacrifice of her two sons.

There is a tree for all of them now. The lantern
guards its grateful forest of the fallen while
across the street cratered asphalt separates
Vimy Ridge from Winners and Canadian Tire.

Cities Within Us

The cross and orb that top the Dresden Frauenkirche were crafted by a British goldsmith whose father took part in the fire raids in February 1945.
—BBC News

Built for a baroque Emperor in his Florence on the Elbe,
the Dresden Frauenkirche stands serenely against a lasting sky
in Canaletto's painting: her graceful dome,
the Stone Bell, hard as Meissen porcelain,
deflecting the impotent cannon balls of invading princes
to rise above a busy marketplace, calling
her faithful to the catechisms of Luther
and eternal anthem of the *Ode to Joy*.

But when they came for her on Ash Wednesday,
unrepentant winged furies dropping
4,000-pound blockbuster bombs with incendiaries
to create das Höllenfeuer,
there was no water for the hoses
or shelters for the people,
only flames and whirlwind and terror.

The dead not cremated in their own homes
were stacked in funeral pyres in the streets
and torched with flamethrowers.

She alone withstood the bombing and the fire
to become a sacred kiln heated above 1000° Celsius,
annealing her faithful to bone ash and eternity,
until dawn's despair awoke her ecstasy
and she collapsed onto
the altar's final sermon in stone.

Her spire cross, twisted into a bombsight,
lay hidden beneath the ruins
for half a century.

Until a new cross, forged in steel
and burnished with gilt by the son of her enemy,
resurrects her random stones to bring
hope and reconciliation to a city
drowned by fire and risen
from the ashes of its mortal clay.

How many died? Who knows the answer?
a great stone asks in silence.

The answer lies within us.
The cities lie within us.

III

Birth Craquelure

And even in our sleep pain that cannot forget
falls drop by drop upon the heart.
—**Aeschylus**, *Agamemnon*

Lineage

My family has a history
of difficult births.

My grandmother's stillborn child
meant my mother would be
the only daughter, and before
they cut me out two months early
they told her I had
strangled myself on the cord.

Three years later,
my sister used the same scar.

After two hours in the delivery room,
they used forceps on my daughter
when her lungs filled
with fluid and we waited
for her to breathe.

It's no coincidence
common names run through my family
like so many birthmarks,
each generation
finds its identity
in the pain of the last.

Outlines

Across this space
words
trade our imaginings
for all reality

we look alike sound alike
smell alike

a candle
in a darkened room

smiling impishly
at the indefinable
that defines us

Like Babies

In prenatal class
we practice the choreography
of a whale colony.

Breathe, says the nurse,
Breathe!—
even husbands holding
to the count of sixty.

The gas in the car never falls
below half a tank. I rehearse
three routes to the hospital
and lie awake at night
thinking of traffic jams.

Each day the suitcase
gets heavier.

But nothing prepares us
for the eruption of life
into our hands,

the ferocity
of a newborn
howling on your belly,
waiting to be named.

And pretty soon
we're all crying
like babies.

A Part of the Family

I've begun a relationship
with my daughter's toys—
they moved in after the birth
and have established
a hierarchy of sorts.

Mr. Moon's impish stare controls
a menagerie of stuffed animals,
their glass eyes revealing
unspeakable desires.

Smile & Suspenders, bookends
with perfect posture,
are looking to take over the shelf.
Even a quiet bath is interrupted
by an impudent turtle
floating by my navel.

The living room is a minefield of Lego.

At night I worry
about the exiles in the garage
who were cuddled and banished
with a kiss.

So, I've adopted them
and wash them
and count them
every night in the drawer.

I've even begun to think
like a toy—choosy in my plastic,
disdainful of batteries, dreaming
of non-toxic happiness,
while all the time readying myself
for the first tell-tale
trumpet call to arms.

Self-Portrait

Saturday morning at the art gallery,
my daughter in the stroller after breakfast,
a chance to talk with no one around
thinking art is better
than cartoons or sleeping in.

Tastes vary. She adores
landscapes, tiny villages, tapestries,
Milne's delicate water colours,
anything with animals.

I prefer abstracts, painting
behind the painting,
when the heart frees itself
and pours space.

We both agree on sculpture,
taut shapes caressing
things we recognize or not.

The Inuit art on the third floor
is always last—

mythic animals
struggling in stone,
caught blood,
moments of light.

Orbit

sand from mars january 6 1989

In the expanding universe of my left kidney,
Calcium Oxalate goes supernova
and creates a new star.
Soon there are tiny planets
in orbit around it.
There must be water.

We have to go in, the surgeon says, it's too big.
I see light shining through a heart-
shaped galaxy on his X-ray
and wonder if he knows the name.

It's just oxygen, a mask says, while
another injects me into
my spacesuit and I awake
adrift
in weightlessness.

How do you feel? a mask says.
Water, I dream.

Tonight, I think we're ready
for Mars, I tell her,
but we have to be back before bed.

My daughter beams.
Tired of dusty moons and comets, she loops
the skipping rope safety line through
our basement chair rockets while I
check fuel levels in the Styrofoam engines.
We close our eyes against radiation
before lift-off.

Drifting past my visor I see the other
astronauts returning
and wonder
if they were ready for Mars.

Water, a mask says,
tethering me with a straw.

Passing through a stillness
that awaits us, we hold hands
on the instrument panel so I can feel
my daughter's tiny course
corrections before we land.

Bend down with me, I tell her,
and we'll bring some back,
handing her the film canister.
Later, she labels and dates
her precious grains.

How do you feel, the surgeon says?
Your star is gone, he beams,
only one tiny fragment left
and he doesn't think
we have to go back.

I drive home wondering
what the label says and if
he will remember the date.

The radio tells me
they are getting closer now,
and building new ships.

I smile knowing
how surprised they will be.
They will find water,
and new stars.

PETER TAYLOR

Theory of Everything

I took it while she wasn't looking,
the photograph, I mean. Not her quick eyes

cleaving the world's indifference; not
the star-believing beads hanging in the doorway

where a cat should be, pawing; but
a single page from her physics notebook

lying open on the desk
creating reality, creating singularity,

the exquisite knowingness
of numbers, raw equations

where words become air, ideas
are fire, and mind

is a conjugation of faces:
noun, verb, subject, object.

Melancholia

At five they gave me
frequent flyer points
for morphine, translucent clouds
that curl into my hand
and exit through scars
in secret places.

Time is invisible; nurses.

I wake entombed
in blankets, a clothespin
on my finger, hands
strangling my arm while
downstairs something broken
floats in a jar
without me.

I'm not dying.
I'm being dismantled.

A Complicated Extraction

Fish-mouthed, puss-kissed, the fanged
monster drains serpent's tooth
purulence into blood boils of pain.

Some parts we abandon, unkind absences
we exit drooling gratitude for a slow
steady pressure with controlled force.

Exodontia, goddess of misery, assuaged,
we go about our clotted lives wondering
what it will mean to be buried everywhere.

Raking Leaves in Wind

Rebellious, my mind skitters
across the lawn in wild abandon,
my hands tugging at wisps cart-
wheeling to joy in other places.

I stand defeated beside piles
disintegrating into undone ideas,
each gust scattering
thoughts beyond my reach.

Waiting to Move In

Today I am adrift, having left
but not moved in. The rain's
blanket wrapped around my shoulders,
I wait outside clutching boxes.

Swift eddies at my feet open worlds
for my distraction. Cardboard softens
as a water-fly crawls heroically onto a twig
and sails through a sidewalk storm.

I stoop to assist and drop
my own responsibilities,
floundering to regain the dry
and honest universe of a home.

Dialysis Ward

for Mary

My last Friday visit to the ward with chocolates
for the nurses, two teas, a newspaper for her nap,
and sterile hands that smell
of apricots and alcohol as I scrub
and enter this miraculous bus station
of broken bodies and machines.

The spectre of my father's illness
a generation before lingers around me.

My first week here I felt as naked as a patient's undone gown,
unsure of what to do or how to help.
Six months along I knew ketosis in a kiss
and could bark *finish your lunch—your sugar sucks!*
for fear my sister's ambulance would be too late.

She loved her giant doctor who, away that day,
now asks what happened. I tell him how
she always said he looked so tearful
when he pulled her tests, they were so bad.
I think he needs a hug, she'd whisper.

I ask about the others.

Normal Bob, his only flaw
a pristine bandage hidden beneath
sleeves creased to perfection; and
Needle Boy, who drove the nurses crazy

pulling needles from his arm
until he bled out two machines.

I heard he did a week in Tower 10 before his code.

And Crazy Jane, whose pinstriped scooter
raced through bedpan alley on the clock,
dusting chairs and gurneys to be the first
for Wheel-Trans in the lot.

All gone now.
Here some get beepers and some just time.

It's raining when I leave, the sun's quiescent glare
refracts to childlike colours—
red orange yellow green blue indigo violet—
I still believe.

Much Ado About Nothing

The worst part was the whispering
in the doorway and my professor telling me
in the middle of tutorial to call home.
Depressed, bipolar, she had done it again:
swallowed everything and just wandered off
into a field with a pillow. Someone noticed
and called the police. The pillow I understood—
go out with a little comfort. But it still seemed
so unfair: not her field and not the play I needed
for exams. All the way home on the bus I felt
banal. Midnight, my stepfather whispers, they'll know
after midnight. His practicality I understood—
me thinking Benedick…*get thee a wife* …
and him saying go out, see a movie.
The Great Escape, again. Hoping this time
they would all get out, this time
he would clear the wire into Switzerland,
this time they wouldn't shoot the fifty.

Leitmotif

Sweet cinnamon red
You're in my head
*   Valproic's not around*

Lamotrigine
You're never mean
*   You keep me on the ground*

But most of all
Haloperidol
*   It keeps my feathers fluffed*

Diazepam
It makes the man
*   I'm glad I have enough*

My Trazodone
I'm all alone
*   O will you marry me?*

And when I can
L-triptophan
*   And happy I will be*

Without my friends
I'm at loose ends
*   Or living on the streets*

But don't despair
There's lots more there
    Keep filling those repeats

Electric Clouds

when is it day when
is it day when is
it day when
is it
day

TAYLOR, Lois, 55, female; sev catatonic st
w compl musc flaccid/motor dys; aware;
prev Rx ineffect; card ok; fam advised risk;
involunt.

mouths are sticks
hands are belts
lights burn
me

ROOM 6-09:15; bilat pulse curr @ 800 mA;
hold +1.5 above seiz thresh; 6 sec; pt sedtd/restr.

cells concatenating railroad explosions ripping through me
arms jerking bands above the table with
me in electric clouds electric
clouds electric
clouds with
no rain

no eyes
in my
head

Rpt. 12, Weds.

jesus this hurts

Christmas in the Ward

The electric bullets in her mind
leave invisible scars
that ricochet in silence.

Ice from a previous winter
forms on the sill where Christmas planters,
primed with bows,
explode crimson from green.

Supper is a show of hands, a vote
for turkey dressing over ham.

The helper ladles pools of cranberries
over stained potatoes, humming a carol
between holly and stainless steel.

Even the Quiet Room is gay,
its lintel broken by a mistletoe.

The key on the hook on the wall
unlocks a door
where mischievous elves
strap presents with gauze and tape
to the tree's exhausted branches.

This is Stephen

And if you had ceased that day
I would not have seen you
Here and understood
The intimate cynicism of the world.
    —Don Coles

I

We all end on a slab somewhere,
open pages from Gray's Anatomy
smelling of ether and formaldehyde,
the final invasion
coming too late.

Your body did not wait
for surgeons and accidents,
its pallid strength spiteful
of itself yet calm
in its resolution
to remain an enigma,
a bruised print.

Brother, where are you?

II

Time
changed you
into ceremonies, kept
the others sane.

My heart shrunk to a fist
with the slow agony
of recognition,
the vague thud
body makes on body
in the comfortless heat
of our embrace.

From the moment
I entered that room,
until the moment
I exit this,

my visitations
between earth
which holds you
and thought
in which you exist.

Time
the idea of space
between words.

III

Midnight faces
explode.

The firemen I called
knowing they respond faster,
choir of sirens
waking the neighbourhood.

Helmets, fire coats, boots
hunched
in that basement room
wanting to be
anywhere else.

I made them use a respirator
even though *rigor mortis*
had begun to set in.

Coroner in evening dress,
a piece of confetti on his collar,
instructs the police
to drive my sister and me
over to tell
your wife and children.

We buy coffee and doughnuts on the way.

IV

I think of dying every day.

Slow excretion of self,
tiny explosions of
heart, brain, kidneys
waiting
to expose the film.

I keep your pictures safe
from the infinite
exposure of the sun.

When I advance
the roll,
you disappear.

Last frame,
carrying your ashes
in a box,

surprised
how little is left.

V

A cold grimace
all you left to the world
and what to me?

You go off,
a flashcube in my head.

Tongue swollen as scream,
face a pale mask
orbiting
my night constellation.

Hand stretches
to touch you
across film, across thought,
tearing illusive
filaments of memory.

In the intimate
sepulchre of existence,
language contaminates
as it creates
the flawed universe
we imagine and inhabit,

turning the print
over and over
in my mind.

Cleaning Stones

These stones are patient sundials waiting
for each hand stroke to clear away the names.

You tidy the grass while I wrench weeds
and plant our solitary flowers.

In an hour we are on the highway
thinking (you laugh) do they hear footsteps?

More caretaker than a pilgrim, more pilgrim than a son,
I scrape clean layers of ancestral soil.

Acknowledgements

Some of these poems originally appeared in *Hell-box* (Frog Hollow Press, 2020). "Mary Agnes Taylor" and "Icarus" originally appeared in *Trainer* (Paget Press, 1980).

Poems have also appeared in the following journals: *Amsterdam Quarterly, Antarctica Journal, Anatomy & Etymology, Aperçus Literary Magazine, A Quiet Courage, Ariel Chart International Literary Journal, Call & Response, Canadian Family Physician, CommuterLit, Contemporary Verse 2, The Copperfield Review, Defenestration: A Literary Magazine Dedicated to Humor, Descant, The Ekphrastic Review, Eunoia Review, Fade, The Font: A Literary Journal for Language Teachers, Forage Poetry Journal, Form Quarterly, FreeXpresSion Australia, The Glass Coin, Harvest, Ink Sweat & Tears, Into the Void, The Linnet's Wings, Nether Quarterly, Open Minds Quarterly, Petrichor Review, Phantom Kangaroo, Pirene's Fountain, Poetry Australia, Pyrta, StepAway Magazine, The Stray Branch, Streetcake Experimental Writing Magazine, Tipton Poetry Journal* and *The Toronto Quarterly*.

Enduring thanks to Laurie Graham, Bruce Hunter, Shane Neilson, Richard Stevenson, and Bruce Whiteman for their generous editorial advice; to Ian Cameron, Leslie Monkman, Michael Ridley, and Richard Spooner as first readers; to Connie Guzzo-McParland, Michael Mirolla, Anna van Valkenburg and the amazing professionals at Guernica Editions; and to my family with affection and gratitude for their love and support, without which many of these poems would never have been written.

Cover image: Andraszy, *Frauenkirche nachts, Dresden 2019* (Wikimedia Commons). Dresden's iconic octagonal Church of Our Lady, destroyed in February 1945, re-built with international support using some of its original sandstone blocks and reconsecrated in October 2005.

13. T.S. Eliot, "Burnt Norton," *Four Quartets*, Faber and Faber: London, 1944. **18.** Diana Cox-Foster and Dennis van Engeldorp, "Solving the Mystery of the Vanishing Bees," *Scientific American*: New York, April, 2009. **41.** Arthur Rimbaud, *A Season in Hell*, translated by Norman Cameron, Anvil Press Poetry: London, 1994. **55.** Ira J. Bach and Mary Lackritz Gray, *A Guide to Chicago's Public Sculpture*, The University of Chicago Press: Chicago, 1983. **60.** C.P. Cavafy, *Collected Poems*, translated by Edmund Keeley and Philip Sherrard, edited by George Savidis, Princeton University Press: Princeton, 1975. **67.** BBC News, June 22, 2004. **71.** Aeschylus, "Agamemnon," cited from *The Greek Way*, Edith Hamilton, W.W. Norton: New York, 1930. **95.** Don Coles, *Landslides: Selected Poems 1975-1985*, McClelland and Stewart: Toronto, 1986.

About the Author

Peter Taylor has published six books and chapbooks and his poems have appeared in *Contemporary Verse 2, Descant, The Ekphrastic Review, Grain, Into the Void, Open Minds Quarterly* and *The Toronto Quarterly*. His writing has been published in Australia, the Caribbean, India, Ireland, the Netherlands, Romania, Singapore, Sweden, the United Kingdom and the United States. His first collection, *Trainer*, a mosaic of poems capturing his father's experience as a pilot during the Second World War, with an introductory poem by Raymond Souster, was called "a work of scholarship and imagination" by John Robert Colombo (*The Globe and Mail*). His experimental verse play, *Antietam*, won honourable mention in the international War Poetry Contest in Northampton, Massachusetts. He holds a master's degree in English Literature from the University of Waterloo and has worked as a printer and bookbinder, medical publisher, institute director and non-profit executive. Born in Edmonton, he lives in Aurora, Ontario.